CHINA

Impressions in verse

C.P. Stone

China: Impressions in verse
Copyright © 2007 by C.P. Stone, All Rights Reserved

Layout
   IRIS Enterprises
   Eveleth, MN

Published by
   Shadow IRIS Book Division
   IRIS Enterprises
   4451 Lakeside Drive
   Eveleth, MN 55734-4400
   www.speravi.com

Printed by InstantPublisher.com

Photo of author and artwork by Danielle B. Stone. Other photos by the author.

No portion of this book may be reproduced, stored in or introduced into a retrieval system, or transmitted, in any form or by any means — including photocopying — without the prior permission of C.P. Stone, except in the case of brief quotations embodied in critical articles or reviews. For information, address inquiries to the publisher.

ISBN: 978-0-9796562-1-7

1. China 2. Poetry 3. Travel 4. Haiku

For my "kids"
Beth, Michele, Suzanne, Mare, Leslie and Mick
Happy trails to all . . . now and then

ACKNOWLEDGEMENTS

Special thanks to my wife, Danielle. She critiqued the writing, helped improve the flow, and gave me ideas — some of them about China and writing. I also appreciate the support of Dorothy Barrère, who helped make travel to China possible. I especially thank Chuck Morello and IRIS Enterprises, for helping with the manuscript formatting and publication niceties. Reviewers included Su Jing, Dorothy Barrère, Fr. Rudolph Pakiz, Elizabeth Stone, Danielle Stone and Doug and Mary Lou Rabb. I also want to thank Master Peng You Lian and the Peng You Taijiquan Association in Thunder Bay, Ontario for exploring publication and marketing options in China and Canada.

CONTENTS

Dedication iii
Acknowledgements v
Contents vii
Photographs viii
Introduction ix

The Great Wall 3
Beijing 7
   Tiananmen Square 8
   Forbidden City 10
   Temple of Heaven 11
   Summer Palace 12
Xi'an 15
   Terra Cotta Warriors 16
Chongqing 19
Yangtze River (Changjiang) By Boat 23
   Lesser Three Gorges 27
   Fengdu (Ghost City) 28
   Three Gorges Dam 29
Shanghai 33
Chinese Culture 39
   Art 39
   Food 42
   Beliefs 44
   This and That 48
Traveling In China 53
About the Author 57

PHOTOGRAPHS

Marble boat, Summer Palace, Beijing 1
The Great Wall, Badaling 2
Temple of Heaven, Beijing. 6
Terra cotta warriors and horses, Xi'an 14
Downtown Chongqing 18
Yangtze River (Changjiang) 22
Shanghai from the Bund 32
Giant cauldron or tripod, Beijing 38
Yangtze dragon boat 52

INTRODUCTION

Why go to China? The plane ride is long, the language difficult, the culture and politics different, and the cost high. Yet China attracts interest as perhaps no other place. China is so different and so much a land of mystery and contrasts that it grabs you — not only while you are there, but before and after you go. A few of the "contrasts", as seen through western eyes: ancient/modern, fastidious/neglectful, honorable/corrupt, creative/conventional, seeking wealth/ignoring the poor, emphasizing health/neglecting health, practical/superstitious, money-wise/mismanaging money, beautiful/squalid, hyperbolic/understated, looking to the future/polluting the present, respectful of the past/destructive of the past, worldly/isolationist, centrally ruled/locally controlled, educated/ignorant.

It can be argued that much of this is in the eye of the beholder, and that a person would find such contrasts anywhere, especially in large countries. Yet I think China exhibits greater and more pervasive disparity. One seeks to understand how such differences came about and why they continue. The initial attraction may be the "otherness" of the place, but the conundrums and paradoxes endure — perhaps more in China than anywhere else.

My wife and I visited China as part of a tour group. If we could do it again for the first time, we would probably look for a smaller group, and one allowing more free time, with less emphasis on "shopping opportunities." But overscheduling and group needs are a trade-off for security, coverage, and time and effort needed to make arrangements, especially if one has not done considerable research and pre-planning. Having had an orchestrated, organized introduction to the country, we are more likely to enjoy less structure on a return trip.

We took photos and kept brief journals, but I wanted to boil down my impressions in writing as well. For this purpose, haiku seemed ideal. Comprised of 17 syllables in three unrhymed lines, haiku originated as an outgrowth of Zen Buddhist meditation in the late 17th century. (Roots were much earlier, and the term "haiku" originated in the late 18th century.) Classical haiku are about nature, in a seasonal context. They may contain different levels of meaning and humor. More contemporary haiku cover a wider range of subjects and stray from the classic five-, seven-, five-syllable lines more often. They also incorporate more humor, in my experience, especially in the western world. Both styles should mostly be readable "in one breath", with a pause after the first or second line.

Haiku have value as a meditation form because they cause you to notice and internalize what is going on around you. Anyone can do haiku; anyone can be a poet! Perhaps you will be encouraged to try after reading this. I also hope that this little book will be of some use to visitors to China who want a very quick look at some things Chinese, or even a brief and partial introduction to the country before the 2008 Olympic Games in Beijing.

may your life be touched
with the great gift of China
sometime and somewhere

CPS
2005

THE GREAT WALL

Then

    Yalu to Tianshan
        over three thousand miles long
            massive Ming structure

    set in rugged hills
        Great Wall defends China
            from foes to the north

    Great Wall also served
        to unite Chinese people
            in one great empire

    two thousand years' work
        symbol of spirit, will and . . .
            single-mindedness

    Ghengis Khan once said
        "strength of wall depends on men"
            men need wills and walls

ancient walks and steps
    rise steeply between thick walls
        a broad, secure path

a raised pathway for
    moving men, equipment, news
        defense can vary

uneven steps, slopes
    frustrate enemy movement
        if accessed at night

changing with the land
    height, width and material
        adapting like life

Now

soaring to the sky
    or plummeting in the fog
        the Wall takes your breath

winding over hills
    a many-angled dragon
        caresses the land

visible from the moon?
    maybe yes, maybe no
        we still wonder

watchtowers built
    on strategic defense sites
        help us fight fatigue

peddlers await you
    on level resting places
        buy on the way down

stench of urine strong
    where peddlers sell goods all day
        can't leave but must go

large flocks of small birds
    fly toward the Wall, shy away
        small invaders stopped

a cheap t-shirt boasts
    "I climbed the Great Wall" . . . why not
        "Great Wall endures all"

BEIJING

capital city
    hub for politics, tourists
        old and new cultures

modern and ancient
    history, mystery, ruling class
        and rush-hour traffic

roofs of golden tile
    protected China's rulers
        in Ming and Qing times

once Peking Man's home
    city of temples and parks
        and modern culture

music, dance and speech
    stylized fine and martial arts
        Beijing Opera

gray and white pigeons
    twisting, turning in town air
        strong flight, gentle birds

    pollution goals set
        to prepare for Olympics
           and foreign critiques

    Beijing Olympics
        will they improve peoples' lives
           even in China?

Tiananmen Square

    one hundred acres
        can hold half a million folks
           largest square in the world

    "the heart of China"
        a focus of government
           kites fly high, hopeful

    Great Hall of People
        sprawls to the west
           Nixon once ate there

    Mao's memorial
        looming east in the gray smog
           past and peddlers there

Heavenly Peace Gate
    seven bridges, five doors north
        central "royalty"

flag ceremonies
    soldiers strut at dawn and dusk
        smaller crowds at dawn

Heroes Monument
    an obelisk from '58
        not for everyone

student strife ignored
    others who "liberated"
        remembered longer

three main holidays
    each worth a week off from work
        Square festivities

fall, winter and spring
    interludes for laborers,
        new year and the nation

Forbidden City

    historians tout
        "the best group of old buildings
            extant in China"

    for five hundred years
        rulers of two dynasties
            lived in seclusion

    an uncommon place
        just not the peasants' domain
            to enter was to die

    eunuchs and officials
        took money, set fires, got rich
            castrated Dragon

    in a darkened room
        Pu Yi, age six, signed away
            "Empire of the Sun"

    city relics lost
        in fires and to Japanese
            some went to Taiwan

    visitors today
        prepare to be touched — and pushed
            but at least not killed

Temple of Heaven

"Tiantan" in Chinese
 three major halls, one altar
  think circles and tiers

the emperor sought
 guidance from the heavens and
  rain and good harvest

lantern on a pole
 signaled emperor's presence
  light sought from above

a circular wall
 echoes the sounds of voices,
  past sacrifices

we climbed a stairway
 three, nine-step tiers of marble
  sacrifice altar

the highest digit:
 nine is odd and from heaven
  so is the altar

and heaven is round
 but the earth is smaller, square
  don't tell Columbus!

    the Abstinence Hall
        purity of motive made
            rulers strong within

    abstain from what things?
        sex, labor and alcohol . . .
            music and garlic!

    beyond the buildings
        azure-winged magpies fly in
            a green grove of trees

Summer Palace

    a royal playground
        beautiful buildings and grounds
            Summer Palace park

    covered corridor
        open-sided, world's longest
            Sistine-like ceiling

    marble Jade Belt Bridge
        arching up with stone railings
            crosses Kunming Lake

a large bronze ox rests
    keeps watch on an island bridge
        and those who cross it

a large marble boat
    part of the empress's fleet
        in the summer, hope floats

tour boats crowd the lake
    a pleasant place now for all
        still fit for royals

XI'AN

"City of the Past"
    ancient dynasties ruled here
        city walls still stand

bell and drum towers
    mark morning and evening hours
        city-center sounds

dragons cause earthquakes
    towers can control dragons
        no recent earthquakes

two Wild Goose pagodas
    store Indian Buddhist scriptures
        sacred T'ang writings

lime green taxi cabs
    wax and wane, both day and night
        a busy "small" town

small brown street workers
    Eurasian tree sparrows clean
        a Chinese habit

T'ang Dynasty show
    dancers' long silk sleeves convey
        feelings gracefully

T'ang music lively
    panpipes, horns, zheng, loud pipa
        and cymbalism

folks gather in park
    to talk, dance, celebrate life
        happy times outside

diverse Xi'an town
    mosque buildings in Chinese style
        many cultures and times

deep in a mosque tree
    laughing thrush scolds all of us
        tourists and monks too

Terra Cotta Warriors

Emperor Qin
    first ruler of all China
        established standards

he finished the Wall
    standardized money, roads, script
        but abused people

Qin feared afterlife
    believed it was under ground
        wanted security

thousands of warriors
    fashioned from terra cotta
        guard his underworld

two hundred bowmen
    and thirty-five chariots
        have so far emerged

figures all differ
    generals, high officials
        bowmen, rank and file

digging continues
    but preserving and storing
        are expensive tasks

found by a peasant
    warriors are China's treasure
        and also the world's

CHONGQING

Chongqing: mountain "town"
   only thirty-five million
      China's big city

five-story bookstore
   avant-garde shopping district
      fine dining downtown

General Stillwell and
   World War II Flying Tigers
      cozy times with U.S.

Peoples' Assembly Hall
   seats four thousand, sounds super
      the pride of Chongqing

Ehrling Park plaza
   manicured and expansive
      favored by locals

slow, graceful movements
   some people play t'ai chi there
      even in midday

Painters' Village art
   "discounts" float higher, higher
      but no bargaining!

Three Gorges Museum
   Yangtze flood depths on wall map
      some towns grow, some go

noise pollution FLASH!
   vehicle horns illegal
      can city folks cope?

Sichuan Province hot
   food and air can make you sweat
      Chongqing hills can too

YANGTZE RIVER (CHANGJIANG) BY BOAT

world's third-longest
    after Nile and Amazon
        Mississippi sixth

major shipping route
    seven-tenths of Chinese trade
        and more with the dam

Changjiang like the Platte
    too thin to plow, thick to drink
        a lot to swallow

water buffalos
    rice paddies, fish ponds, egrets
        Yichang countryside

Yangtze dragon boat
    four decks, eighty-seven rooms
        not Huck Finn's raft trip

wood of lacquered red
   cozy rooms, each with shower
   and a balcony

dragon boats honor
   reformer-poet who drowned
   in river, despair

a lion dance for us
   bright costumes, drums and tea
   a different world

boat dock at pre-dawn:
   metal walkways clang and squeak
   men shout in the dark

rain blurs lights at night
   green for buoys, yellow on hills
   as boat steams upstream

morning rain still falls
   t'ai chi on an open deck
   wet moving stillness

clinging to hillsides
   sesame, corn, lotus, gourds
   small fields, many shapes

scarecrows in corn fields
    bright red — a joyful color
        scare monkeys and birds

trucks along the way
    dump coal on ramps for barges
        dam power comes soon

water-level marks
    predict future water height
        and the depth of loss

abandoned buildings
    stand alone or in large groups
        soon to be submerged

sculling with one arm
    rowing with the other one
        stern sampan woman

Qutang, Wu, Xiling
    beautiful misty gorges
        uplift and inspire

egrets, small and white
    spaced along the Yangtze banks
        shoreline sentinels

look! two large white birds
    fly over a distant town
        maybe they were cranes

dragon(flies) still rule
    over Changjiang, river towns
        the warm air is full

barn swallows swoop down
    catch dragonflies on the wing
        which is yin, which yang?

dawn and dusk darters
    bats capture some mosquitoes
        bring us good fortune

dead pig floats downstream
    bloated, stiff, turning slowly
        legs high on the hog

men with large, fine nets
    scoop the brown Yangtze waters
        seeking food or junk?

high on the skyline
    a cross silhouette far off
        distant reminder

Lesser Three Gorges

    Lesser Gorge water
        green and clear — not silty brown
            like Yangtze River

    cedar-hulled sampans
        with woven bamboo roofs, powered
            by poles or motors

    riverman poles boat
        coat of fur to warm shoulders
            cone hat of white straw

    sampan boatmen sing
        songs of the river of old
            voices clear and high

    music echoes down
        as sampan glides quietly by
            flute player on hill

    sitting in small groups
        on rocks or sometimes in trees
            golden-haired monkeys

    missed the mandarins
        they really ducked out on us
            Lesser Gorge downer

ancient "hanging graves"
    in stone caves high on gorge walls
        heaven close up there

bodies down on ropes?
    was the water higher then?
        no one knows for sure

"trackers" lean upstream
    ropes on shoulders, pulling boats
        bucking current trends

Fengdu (Ghost City)

Pingdu Mountain site
    king of netherworld lived here
        now a ghost garden

a submerged ghost town
    dammed river displaces spirits
        will they relocate?

peddlers riverside
    and high above the Changjiang
        remote tourist trap

    hundreds of steps up
        temples of three major faiths
           plus some folk beliefs

    fun tests for tourists
        what does future hold for you?
           come see . . . for a price

    lush vegetation
        along the steep trail to top
           nice views of Changjiang

    cicadas vibrate
        whining from trees all around
           can't find even one!

    quiet behind a leaf
        thick ivory bill, black head
           collared finchbill sits

Three Gorges Dam

    dam for flood control,
        power and navigation
           Shanghai gets power

planet's largest dam
    fifteen hundred meters wide
        sixteen years to build

five locks raise vessels
    six hours to pass through each way
        slow boat in China

Three Gorges Center
    neat and clean for tourist crowds
        looks down on the dam

along nature trail
    large hoopoe feed on the ground
        flutter to bamboo

white wagtail on shore
    a long-tailed, black and white bird
        hunts bugs by a dam site

long-tailed shrike hunts too
    familiar large head, hooked bill
        alert for small prey

no greenhouse gases
    with hydropower — but silt,
        leaks occur with time

untreated sewage
    toxins from past and present
        other concerns flow

once the dam is done
    can Chinese sturgeon still spawn
        river dolphin live?

so much water stopped
    will earth's balance be thrown off?
        butterfly wings flap . . .

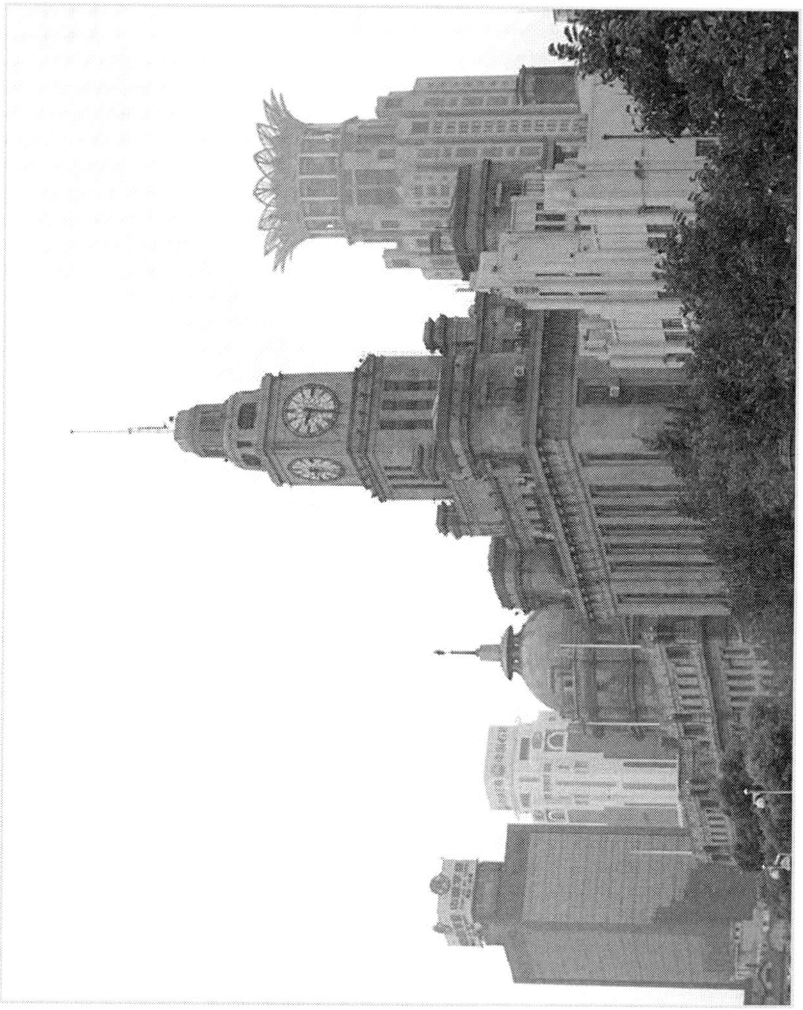

SHANGHAI

Shanghai: once reckless
   with men's lives and fortunes
      now features shopping

from fishing, weaving
   to vice, ship building, commerce
      Shanghai changes fast

transplanted camphor,
   magnolia, sycamores
      propped up everywhere

tall construction cranes
   in flocks throughout the city
      show off rapid growth

"City of the Future"
   Shanghai is world commerce town
      major port of call

bicyclists pulling
   carts with impossible loads
      in heavy traffic

bright yellow taxis
    swarming and bunching like ants
        seen from hotel heights

how can two objects
    occupy same space, same time?
        drive Shanghai and see!

bustling all night long
    bikes crisscross moving car lights
        dark figures on foot

noisy cars and trucks
    horns constantly sounding off
        is there a beep code?

two honks — I'm passing
    one honk — watch out, coming fast
        three honks — thanks? Fat chance!

architecture great!
    buildings like gourds, pliers, pots
        old and new mishmash

shaped like space needle
    hotel has "rooms in the clouds"
        and sky-high prices

buildings with high holes
    ample for dragon fly-throughs
        that bring good fortune

Shanghai Museum
    kettle-like structure outside
        inside, culture brews

waterfront buildings
    supported on concrete rafts
        and water beneath

the Bund (waterfront)
    go at night to shop or view
        then you'll see the light

Typhoon Matsa blows
    trees bend, rain comes in hard sheets
        lights out in the Bund

Jade Buddha Temple
    pungent incense, worshippers
        imposing statues

large Burmese Buddha
    jade luster glows as he sits
        skin pale in low light

Yu Yuan Gardens
    buildings, ponds, rocks and statues
      vintage Ming and Qing

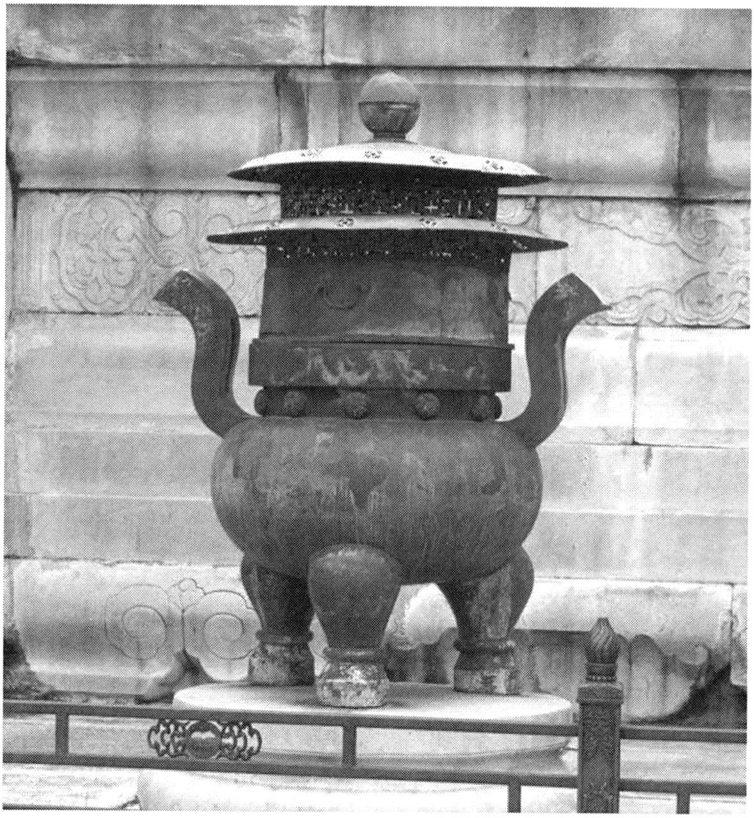

CHINESE CULTURE

Art

    paintings in bottles,
        on silk, leaves, paper and wood
            some common substrates

    ship in a bottle?
        picture an entire landscape!
            snuff bottle paintings

    using a curved brush
        artist paints snuff glass inside
            the patience of Job

    better art with age
        son, father and grandfather
            experience tells

    ink finger-paintings
        depict majestic mountains
            rising from Yangtze

water, ink, paper
    side of hand and fingernails
        slight of hand landscape

strokes done in order,
    with ink brush and steady hand
        calligraphy art

silkworms spin out silk
    many strands make one strong thread
        threads make clothes and rugs

silk clothing creates
    skin and silk interaction
        healthful slinkiness

worms boiled in water
    made into our cosmetics
        or our medicines

embroidered silk cloth
    no right or wrong side to view
        such a two-faced art

copper strips, plant glue
   paint, fire many times, polish
      cloisonné warms heart(h)s

giant bronze cauldrons
   many uses, show one's status
      emperor used nine

ancient jade carvers
   made useful tools, utensils
      now small and large art

color, rarity
   hardness and artist's skill
      "price for gold, not jade"

"scenic openings"
   ornate window and door shapes
      frame views in and out

kites: art, pastime, luck
   bright colors, many sections
      brighten windy sky

Food

    food brought to table
        one dish after another
            meal ends with the soup

    lazy Susan style
        food rotated by diners
            watch when, what you spin

    chopsticks held right
        may well grasp most food items
            but chin bowl for rice

    "you'll like chicken feet"
        and chicken served many ways
            maybe chopped, bones and all!

    chef carves duck dinner
        each thin piece with skin and meat
            sesame bun, bean paste

    round moon cakes stuffed with
        meat, nuts, fruits; flavored, seasoned
            a heavenly treat

    dumplings, boiled or steamed,
        may be shaped like what's inside
            or you eat, then learn

Sichuan food the best!
   dishes multiply, room hot
      bring more beer!

Tsingtao beer, green tea
   Sprite, water (boiled or bottled)
      Chinese beverages

compress or ferment
   drink natural or scented
      tea soothes, relaxes

different teas cure
   many different maladies
      wake or sleepify

Tsingtao beer so mild
   goes with food, found all over
      drink beer, not water!

<u>not</u> made in China
   never saw fortune cookies
      ate dozens of meals

Beliefs

    placate ancestors
        a moral life brings good luck
            divine the future

    raised threshold blocks way
        evil spirits can't jump over
            step left, then step right

    thresholds block evil
        trip up those who don't watch out
            as do our beliefs

    giant bronze phoenix
        symbol of good relations
            renewed and stable

    kites dart, swoop and soar
        colorful, artistic and . . .
            carry off bad luck

    fish scales, deer antlers
        eagle claws, goat head, shrimp eyes
            dragons guard the land

dragon is China
   large, old, powerful, diverse
      heating up within?

dragons represent
   ch'i — vital life energy
      and that in cosmos

dragon claws stand for
   water, metal, wood, earth, fire
      essentials for life

dragons need five toes
   just three or four unlucky
      at least in China

feng shui — arranging
   watch the placement, in and out
      use stones and mirrors

feng shui teaches
   human surroundings matter
      good placement and times

mind, body, spirit
   sense water, hills, wind and more
     best to plan for it

tranquil gardens, parks
   control human surroundings
     renew our spirits

architecture too
   in harmony with nature
     real or created

most vehicles have
   feng shui tassles or symbols
     and for good reason!

feng shui animals
   dragon horse, unicorn, lion
     bring good luck to you

rub a dragon horse
   both hands for ears, whiskers, feet
     wings and rump — the end!

paired lions guard buildings
   lucky feng shui creatures
     just a little pride

female lion to left
    ears and mouth closed, head is down
        paw on supine cub

male lion to the right
    ears and mouth open, head up
        paw resting on world

that's upon entry
    but if you're leaving building
        females must be right

roof ridge animals
    conjure rain to put out fires
        numbers show status

so many symbols
    happiness, long life, health, wealth
        hopes for now and then

huge Buddhas of gold
    enlightened or becoming
        but then, aren't we all?

    reclining Buddha
        facing death at peace, tranquil
            gives hope to viewers

    Buddha hands say
        "protect you", "grant you favors"
            or teach you doctrine

    joss sticks and incense
        red candles in tripod pots
            Buddhist temple prayers

    incense and candles
        deliver prayers heavenward
            contributions help

This and That

    silk and paper fans
        used to cool faces . . . still do
            way cool, even now

    against sun and rain
        umbrellas open from buds
            like lovely flowers

Chinese language sings
   delightful to listen to
      hard to learn the score

words can have four tones
   up, down, flat or changing
      a little means much

paper currency
   different sizes and colors
      metal coins are few

Chinese do not like
   things out of place — pick it up,
      turn it off, right now

polishing, cleaning
   exception: Chinese toilets
      smelly, yucky, wet

peng, chow and mah jong!
   circles, characters, bamboos
      dragons, winds, seasons

such a pretty game!
   tiles of ox bone and bamboo
      build your own Great Wall

willows along banks
    beautifully soften and hide
        drab drainage canals

where is the blue sky?
    viewscapes everywhere are lost
        pictures capture "haze"

industries that pollute
    just moved to city outskirts
        out of sight and mind

Mao's "Little Red Book"
    in plastic, bilingual
        old thoughts, new wrappers

a Chinese saying
    "Mao right seventy percent"
        still much honored there

"hecho in China"
    globalization is here
        does Wal-Mart approve?

"little emperors"
   China's one-child policy
      praised and criticized

income gap growing
   fewer young support more old
      "enemy is us"

dissent not allowed
   people displaced, moved off land
      economics rule

still, "mountains are high,
   the emperor far away"
      power is local

rebuilding structures
   that rulers, foreigners razed
      honors the past

but rebuilding can
   also rewrite past history
      few ancient ruins here

China and Japan
   thoughts stuck on past, no love lost
      human weaknesses

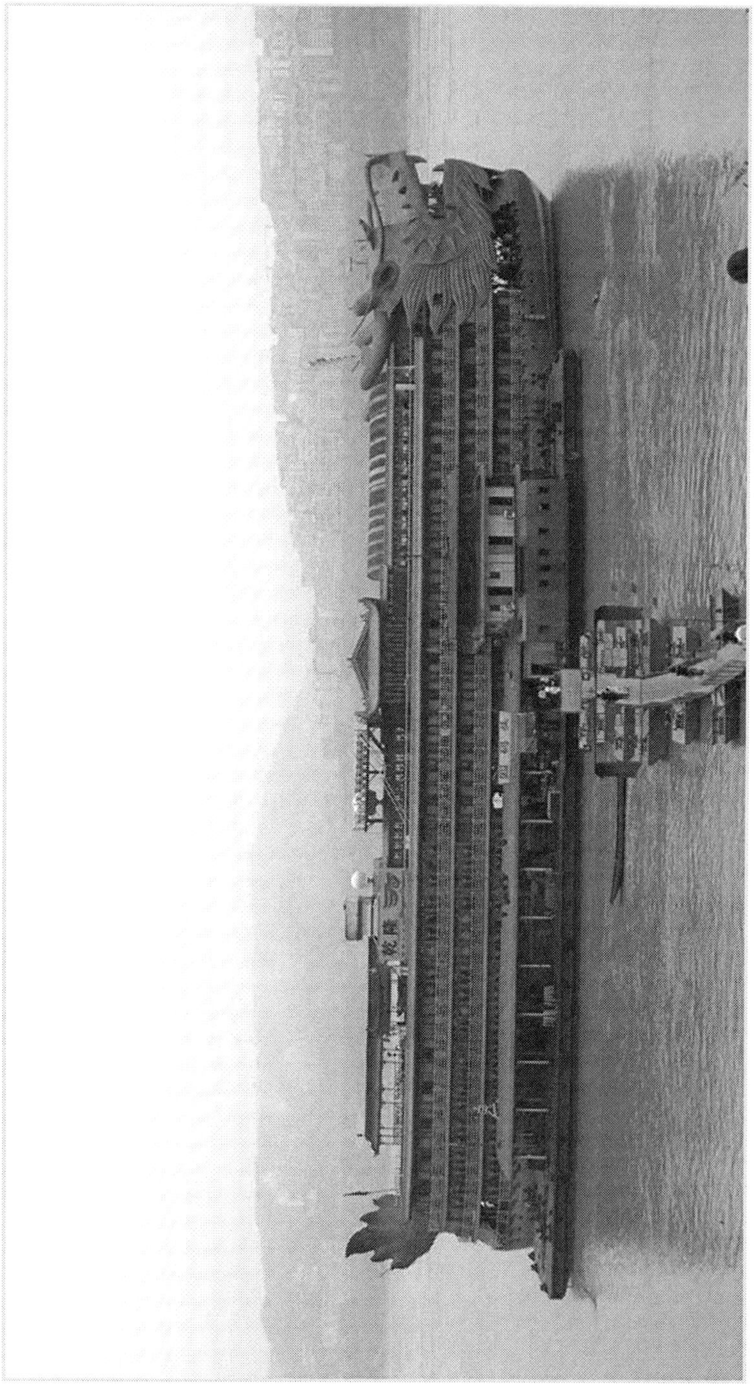

TRAVELING IN CHINA

preparing for weeks
    foreign travel weight limits
        just too much to take

we're off to China!
    wing across the Pacific
        exotic land calls

don't drink the water
    nose, mouth and eyes off limits
        sanitize your hands

add some hot water
    for instant noodle soup with
        tiny fork as prize

sales folks follow us
    our every gesture and word
        a clue to our thoughts

peddlers, beggars and
    handicapped people draw close
        it's need more than greed

really want to buy
    or is bargaining the game?
        dealer's choice or yours

dvd's a buck
    bargains are found everywhere
        street shoppers beware

buy something awkward?
    mail it to final hotel
        more room on flight home

tour guides give us facts
    highest, oldest, most and best
        proud of their country

sometimes fewer facts
    more time to enjoy sights, sounds
        would be more fitting

thousands of dollars,
    miles, and much prep time for just
        "ten minutes free time"

guide megaphones drone
    as do some guides. "China loud"
        Chinglish puzzling too

folks enter photo
    push "delete" and start again
        a digital world

a Chinese challenge
    kung fu toilets: assume stance
        bring your own paper

diarrhea strikes
    no paper in W. C.
        Chinese invention

to get place to place
    China's trains beat planes for price
        much local motion

"hard sleepers" are seats
    "soft sleepers", bunks in a room
        with a moving view

train travel at night
    allows more daytime shopping
        but landscapes are missed

ABOUT THE AUTHOR

C.P. (Chuck) Stone is a retired research biologist who lives at the "end of the road" near Ely, MN with his good and talented wife, Danielle. His parents and three universities attempted to educate him, but he went to work for the Federal government anyway. He led research teams and conducted his own research, chiefly to reduce "problem" species and enhance survival of rarer forms. He is senior author of two books, senior editor of three others and of numerous symposia, and author or coauthor of well over a hundred scientific and popular articles. Research activities took him to Mexico, Canada, New Zealand, Guam and the Marianas, and the Galapagos Islands, as well as most U.S. states.

Chuck has taught adult religious and environmental education, and presently teaches several t'ai chi classes of different levels and styles with his wife. He has studied taijiquan since 2000, with a number of masters and instructors from China, Canada, Australia and the U. S. He enjoys canoeing and kayaking, skiing and snowshoeing, reading and writing, birding, photography, and a bunch of other stuff. Six children consider him a parent so far, and he is grandfather to six smaller life forms. He is blessed by all of the above.